WICCA FOR BEGINNERS

A GUIDE TO RITUALS, BELIEFS, AND WICCAN MAGIC

By K. Connors

Table of Contents

INTRODUCTION 4

CHAPTER ONE 6

ABOUT WICCA 6

CHAPTER TWO 15

WHAT IS WICCA REALLY? 15

CHAPTER THREE 21

THE HISTORY OF WICCA 21

CHAPTER FOUR 32

GUIDANCE FOR WICCA BEGINNERS 32

CHAPTER FIVE 45

STEPS FOR BEGINNERS 45

CHAPTER SIX 53

WICCAN SYMBOLS 53

CHAPTER SEVEN 59

THE WICCAN CALENDAR 59

CHAPTER EIGHT 68

MODERN WICCA 68

CLOSING REMARKS 71

INTRODUCTION

If you are thinking about beginning your journey down the Wiccan path, it is helpful to know what you will need to get started. This beginner's guide is designed to help you as a you get started on your spiritual journey.

The first thing that any witch should understand are the five elements. The four basic elements are earth, water, fire, and wind. These elements represent every physical aspect of our experience in this physical form.The fifth element is referred to in many different ways including the void, akasha, and spirit. The fifth element is the aspect of us that connects, relates, and uses the physical elements. Everything is made up of water, earth, fire, wind, or a combination of those elements. You must learn more about these elements if you wish to develop any form of power.

Any good Wicca beginner's guide will also tell you that an understanding of plants, herbs, minerals, and colors is also essential. These are used in many different spells and each has its own ability. A good understanding of plants and herbs is especially important as these will become your caldron staples harvested from nature's bounty for your use in spells, tinctures, and the like. In fact, long ago, many women were burned at the stake because of their understanding of plants and their natural healing applications.

The next step on the path must start with the procurement of a reference library. Anyone on a spiritual path stands to benefit from a teacher, a mentor, or a guide. Books are the quickest and easiest way to obtain the needed knowledge. A good library or online collection of books such as Amazon, will help you to learn the foundations of Wiccan practices and provide reference material for plants, herbs, minerals, and energies found in nature. If you are to harness the energies of nature, you must first be able to identify them. Start building your reference library now.

CHAPTER ONE

ABOUT WICCA

Wicca is a neopagan form of witchcraft. Due to the stigma that is attached to the word 'witch' (built over centuries from persecution and distortion of reality), the term Wicca is preferred in modern times. The degree in which you adhere to the ancient ways is a matter of choice and there is much confusion as to how much we know of the original ways anyway. Many are happy to follow a modern, updated faith, safe in the knowledge that it's in keeping with the original values. An example of this would be that most Wiccans write spells in the modern tongue. This is because it is easier for us to understand and, therefore the energies we can create are more powerful as a result. At the same time, the spirits of the universal elements that our forbearers called upon many years ago are still central, so there is a balance.

No introduction to Wicca could fail to mention the universal elements of fire, air, water, earth, and spirit. These are the universal elements that make up the recognizable Wiccan symbol of the pentacle. Within these elements are the spirits of the universe's power. Wiccans look to these powers as part of their rituals, to complement their spell work, or as a part of their festivals. It is a celebration of nature and the power we can create by being in harmony and at one with the natural world.

Wiccans believe that energies are male and female - separate in their identities, powerful in their union. They are honored equally. The twin deities of the God and Goddess are represented in many ways and forms, but are central to the Wheel of Life, a cycle that is in tune with the seasons. The Goddess gives birth to the God, who grows as she rests. When the God is fully grown, he and the Goddess then fall in love and she then becomes pregnant. As she grows with the child, the God wanes and dies only to be reborn again. These stages are all celebrated throughout the year in the 8 Wiccan festivals.

Many Wiccans permanently identify with a particular deity, while others will call upon a God or Goddess with the relevant powers for their particular spell only. Some choose not to do either. There are virtually no rules to Wicca and for many of its followers this is its greatest.

However, an introduction to Wicca should include the basic principle that should be at the heart of all of your work, worshipping, and beliefs: An it harm none, do as ye will.

When seeking an introduction to Wicca, many are in fact just intrigued by spell casting! Spells are not essential to all Wiccans, but for those that do include them in their lifestyle, it is part of honoring and respecting the world around us rather than attempting to create miracles. Casting a spell is an emotional act and requires an appreciation of the energies that exist in the natural universe in order to feel them shift and to move with them.

It is always best to start off with something simple and to try to master this before moving on to anything more complex. You're also likely to start off with something written by another, but most find that your own spells, including those adopted by you for your needs, are the most effective. Finding the right combinations of natural ingredients, tools that you can connect with, the right words to help you tune into the right spirits, and powers both within and around you is, for many, one of the most life-affirming aspects of Wicca.

THINGS TO KNOW ABOUT WICCA

If you're just starting along your spiritual path this can be very daunting even scary at times. When you are seeking knowledge, who should you believe? I will offer one sound piece of advice, "Don't believe everything that you read, but always follow your own intuition". If something feels wrong or that little voice inside your head is saying, "No way", then by all means, listen! Here are some real facts about Wicca and common questions that may help you along your path to universal truth and enlightenment.

1. **Wicca is a real religion.** Wicca is a protected religion by the United States Constitution. There are Wiccans that serve openly in the US military. There are many variations on how to practice Wicca. Wicca is an earth-based religion. Followers believe in the elements, the god and goddess, different types of supernatural beings, and so much more.

2. **Wicca is a structured religion, but there are not extreme guidelines.** Yes, there are basic rules that most all Wiccans follow, but nothing is truly etched in stone. Every person who practices Wicca has their

own guidelines and rules, as well as their own beliefs, customs, spell works, practices, and divinities that they prefer to work with. As you continue your Wicca studies, it is entirely up to you to decide what feels right to you and to identify your true spiritual needs.

3. **Most Wiccans follow a moral and ethical code.** If someone you know says that they are Wiccan, they follow the Wiccan Rede, and they practice black magic; their statement is an oxymoron. When one practices black magic they work with entities that are dark and dangerous, such as demons. When someone plays with black magic they can be pulled into the darkness before they even realize that they have been taken. Wicca mimics Native American beliefs, such as all living things are sacred, and most Wiccans do not cast spells that will harm another person. Many practitioners believe in the Wiccan Rede which states, **"An ye harm none, Do what ye will"**.

4. **Is there an afterlife?** Some Wiccans believe there is an afterlife and others do not. Most Wiccans believe in reincarnation. Gerald Gardener wrote that the Summerland is a resting place for the souls until they are reborn. Most Wiccans believe that

mediums and psychics can reach across the great divide and speak to our lost loved ones and other all-knowing and all-seeing entities.

5. **What about discrimination and social feedback?** If you decide that Wicca is where your spirituality lies, it will be time to decide if you will live an open life as a Wiccan or stay in the broom closet, so to speak. You must keep in mind that there is still a plethora of close-minded views on the Wiccan religion. Here are a few questions you should ask yourself before deciding to live an open, honest, and free Wiccan lifestyle.

Am I financially independent? If your parents still pay your bills, then the answer is no. Will you be cut off emotionally and financially? If your parents are practicing Christians, this could happen! Always think before you act. Be yourself, always, but also put yourself in a position to succeed. When you are financially stable, there is nothing stopping you from living freely, out in the open, just as you are. However, for many this may not be a reality, so be wary until you know you can hold your own in the world.

Can I lose my job? In most cases you shouldn't, but it is still very rough terrain for the average Wiccan. Ask yourself, "Can I prove that I was fired because of my religious beliefs"? If yes, then by all means, come out and defend your right to religious freedom. Know your company's policy and be aware of your rights as an employee. It is up to the employee to provide proof of discrimination. Get proof if you decide to go this route.

6. **Wiccans do not worship the devil.** The devil is dark. The core belief in traditional Wicca is that of light and there is no gray area. Many people assume Wiccans and witches worship dark entities and will do harm against you such as turn you into a toad, give you bad juju, or cast a curse on you. Let's say you have a ruler on a 12-inch scale, with the one end being those who worship Satan/the devil; all the way to the end of the twelfth inch is where Wiccans would be listed. Wiccans do not worship dark entities or the devil.

7. **New witches should use spells and rituals already produced by others.** Well, the truth is yes and no. For many new witches, it seems impossible for them to write their own rituals and spells. If you do not feel confident in writing your own, then you

should find a ritual or spell in a book or online and make it your own. A very important aspect of becoming a Wiccan is that you understand that you are capable; you can succeed at anything that you put your effort and spirit into. If something feels right to you, but others say it is not right or won't work, then you should look at all of the aspects and then do what you feel is right. A great philosophy here is, "To Thine own self be true". You must feel at ease and focused, not unsure and haphazard. Spirituality comes from within, your magic comes from the powers that be, and your determination comes from your strong heart. Never doubt yourself or your beliefs as these things make us tangible; they make us all eternal. They are the very essence of what we are.

8. **Should you do solitary worship and magic or would you be more comfortable in a coven?** Are you more comfortable on your own? Does your magic feel stronger when you're alone or is it intensified when there are others involved? For many, joining a coven helps because they can finally be around others who share their path, and have similar experiences and ideas as they do. For some, it seems that the structure of a coven feels very

inviting. For others, joining a coven feels restricting and chaotic to them. Only you can answer these questions about yourself.

9. **Does it cost a lot of money?** Many new practitioners of Wicca are under the misconception that they have to spend thousands of dollars on ritual and spellcraft tools. This is simply not true. When you are just starting out you can use items from around your home. Please make sure to cleanse any tools that you decide to use as this will release any negative energies and will amplify your rituals and spell effectiveness. If you would like to simplify your spell and ritual craft, work with candle spells or sigil spells. Both can be easily concealed if you are not out yet and they offer minimal material cost and can help you build your working knowledge of magic on a shoestring budget.

CHAPTER TWO

WHAT IS WICCA REALLY?

Wicca is often mistaken for Witchcraft. The truth of the matter is, Wicca is a religious faith all its own. What might surprise people even more is that Wicca is a very loving religious practice; one that demands its followers to adhere to strict ethics and high moral standards. Summed up, these ethics convey the Wiccan Law of "Harm None", which ensures those of Wiccan faith are consistently mindful of their daily actions and resulting effects, and their interactions with mankind, animals, and the environment in which we live.

Wicca incorporates a combination of religious beliefs and practices in its studies. These include; Eastern Philosophy, Mystical Quabalah, and old European traditions. From Eastern Philosophy, Wicca derives its belief system of Cause and Effect, Karma and Reincarnation. The Quabalah lends its principles of Spiritual Evolution through 'path-working', as well as Esoteric Knowledge. And, from

European tradition, Wicca receives its passions and understandings of nature and many of its Deities.

WHAT DO WICCANS WORSHIP?

The foundation of Wicca is based on the belief that there are many forms of 'Divine Spirit' which reside with us here on Earth, as well as in 'Heavenly' Realms, all of which are benevolent, and accessible by mankind to assist us with our needs - both physical and spiritual. Many of these Divine Beings are found in Nature - the elements, the sky, and the Earth 'Herself'.

HOW DO WICCANS WORSHIP?

Wiccans base their primary observances on what is referred to as 'The Wheel of the Year'. This Wheel contains eight sections of time in each year where the changes of the seasons are celebrated by Ritual in order to pay tribute for the gifts and opportunities inherent in each season. Examples include, the asking for protection and needs to be met during winter months, the 'calling forth' of spring (seed and planting time), and giving thanks for crop abundances in the autumn.

WHAT ARE "WICCAN TOOLS" AND WHY ARE THEY USED?

During festivals, Wiccans use ritual tools to assist them with their performances. These include athames, wands, chalices, bowls, candles, and pentacles. Most all of these items correlate with an element of nature, and each has a specific purpose to aid in rituals that are often performed to portray the roles which Divine Spirits play in interacting and impacting our daily lives. Wiccans also use divination tools, such as crystal balls, pendulums, and Tarot cards for seeking spiritual advice and gaining insight into the future.

WICCA AND MAGIC

Much of the misconceptions about Wicca stem from its practice of performing 'magic'. This magic is often (wrongfully) attached to some type of devil-worship by those who do not take the time to research the facts. In truth, most Wiccans do not even believe in a devil. And, if they did, the Code of Ethics and Principles of Wicca would require its followers to stand clear of "him". Again, Wicca promotes well-being unto all.

THE ORIGINS OF MAGIC

The art of performing magic dates back to prehistoric man, when tokens of appreciation were offered during semi-rituals by the tribe in hopes of being granted particular blessings from the Gods of old. The most commonly documented Gods of that era were the Fertility Goddesses and the Gods of the Hunt, both of which were honored frequently in exchange for food and safety.

MAGIC TODAY

Today, much of the makings of magic in Wicca are based on the same platform. Celebrations, dances, and feasts are performed to pay honor to a particular Divine Spirit in exchange for blessings which are bestowed upon the practitioner.

Crafts are made and tokens are offered in the same fashion. These magics range from elaborate gatherings of Wiccan multitudes to the less casual practices of solitary Wiccans, whereas an individual (or group of a few) will perform smaller rituals to gain more personal-type blessings.

OTHER TOOLS OF CRAFT

It is believed by Wiccans that most all natural materials, from stones to plants, withhold specific 'energies' which may be utilized in magic as additional aids for attaining specific results. The most popular of natural materials is perhaps the usage of herbs. Herbs are incorporated into magic by way of making crafts out of them for offerings and tokens of appreciation and honor. Herbs are incorporated into magical workings for their large variety of pleasing fragrances, and for this reason, are commonly used in incense -- which is burned during all religious ceremonies in an effort to attract and compliment the Divine Spirits.

Wicca, throughout the past many years, has done much in the way of promoting religious tolerance in the public's eye. It is not within the religious practice of Wicca to solicit new members or reform those of other religious creeds, but rather to teach by example the many blessings bestowed upon those who abide by the Laws of Love.

Each of the great religions of the world are based on the teachings of making personal improvements and rising above our environments, helping those in need, and becoming more spiritually evolved. It seems impossible, therefore, that any particular creed could be right or wrong with so many parallels and similarities.

CHAPTER THREE

THE HISTORY OF WICCA

The history of Wicca or "The Craft" is complex, but traditional Wicca is rooted in the so-called "British Mystery Traditions", for example, the Picts, who existed before the rise of Celtic consciousness, the Celts, and some Celtic Druidism.

Wicca predates Christianity by about 28,000 years. A variety of archaeological discoveries reveal that the history of Wicca can be traced as far back as the Paleolithic peoples who worshipped a Hunter God and a Fertility Goddess. Cave paintings that are dated at around 30,000 years old depict a man with the head of a stag, and a pregnant woman standing in a circle with eleven other people.

Modern American Wicca has its roots in British Wicca, brought to the United States in the late 1950's by English and American initiates of Gardnerian, Alexandrian and Celtic Wicca. These are merely different forms of Wiccan tradition. All of these cultures form part and parcel of the history of Wicca.

The ancient Greek Mysteries of Eleusis, Italian Mysteries of Rome, Etruria and the general countryside, Mysteries of Egypt and Persia before Islam, and various Babylonian, Assyrian and other mid-eastern Mysteries, also find a place in the history of Wicca, its beliefs, and its traditional practices. Perhaps the best way to describe Wicca is to call it a modern religion that is based on ancient witchcraft traditions, but do bear in mind that not all those who practice witchcraft today are Wiccans.

Wicca is both a belief system and a way of life. Over the years information about how Wiccan ancestors lived and worshipped has been lost due to actions of the medieval church. However, modern Wiccans have tried to reconstruct the history of Wicca in an effort to lay the foundation for their practices.

During ancient times, Wicca was called "The Craft of the Wise". This name was derived from the fact that most Wiccans aligned themselves with the forces of nature. They also had knowledge of herbs and medicines, gave council, and were important in the village community as leaders and Shamanic healers.

The history of Wicca indicates that Wiccans once had a prized place in society which is quite a contrast to how they are viewed today.

Ancient Wiccans felt that man was not superior to nature, the earth, and its creatures. Instead, they were only one aspect of the world. The idea of sustainable development to maintain balance and equilibrium was central to the belief systems of the ancient Wicca. The historical views of Wicca are a far cry from the way that man views the earth and the natural world today.

In the last several hundred years, witchcraft and witches have been incorrectly labeled as evil or unrighteous. Where do these ideas that form so much a part of the history of Wicca originate? Some Wiccans believe that the medieval church of the 15th through 18th centuries created these myths in an effort to convert more people to Christianity. The history of Wicca contains many stories of the persecution of witches based on so-called "evil" practices.

Another theory about the history of Wicca is that as medical science became more prominent in society those who did these initial studies did not understand female physiology, especially menstruation. This "mystery" seemed to fit in with the churches agenda in labeling healers as evil heathens and placing power and respect in the hands of male physicians.

Many of these myths and superstitions have survived in modern times giving the Craft a bad name. While Wicca is essentially witchcraft, those who practice it usually do not refer to it as such because of these negative connotations. The history of Wicca is important since it is the persecution of those who practiced it that has led to its current ethic of "religious freedom first".

WICCA AND WITCHCRAFT

One can be very confused with the modern ideas present today. In fact, a lot of individuals are so involved in their own lives that they do not even bother to think where these modern popular beliefs came from. Modern constructs, such as religion, politics, warfare, and even the internet all originated somewhere, and it is important that people know at least a little about the history of something before they incorporate it as a part of their everyday life.

Take the case of Witchcraft and Wicca; while most people would probably combine these two in the same area of interest such as witchcraft and spells with the occasional magical tool such as the voodoo doll, one might be surprised that Wicca is actually a religion and witchcraft a variant that originated in the Wiccan movement.

Wicca is a modern pagan religion and is concentrated on a more peaceful, harmonious, and balanced way of life. It is a belief system that has pre-Christian origins and details how our ancestors lived and worshipped. It is known to be one of the oldest belief systems in the world today and is generally frowned upon by the modern Christian church due to the strong influence of magic and occultism that was generally present in its practices. Like most of the belief systems that are generally frowned upon by Christians, Wiccan practices carry a deeper meaning that is more concentrated on the worship of the believed gods and goddesses as well as an emphasis on nature. Wicca is originally known as "The craft of the Wise". The general practices involve finding the balance between man and nature and understanding that man and the different elements he has created are only elements of nature.

IS WICCA SAFE?

Wicca, as with all of the various belief and spirituality systems, is perfectly safe. If you get past all of the witchcraft and spells that are closely affiliated with the religion, you can find that they concentrate on a harmonious relationship between themselves and nature. It is against nature to cause harm to anything or anyone and is therefore not the intent of Wiccans in any case.

Various depictions of witchcraft and Wicca make the public believe that it is a cult of satanic worshippers who do nothing but cast curses and hexes on other individuals using magic spells, cause harm to individuals using various magical tools such as voodoo dolls, or engage in various animal and human sacrifices. This is extremely far from the truth as Wicca does not engage in any of these practices. They acknowledge the divine, but they do not advertise themselves as religious leaders to be followed by people in search of spirituality, nor do they claim to worship Satan or demons. Satan and demonic entities are exclusively created by Christianty and are wrongly associated with Wicca and Witchcraft.

WHAT DO WICCANS BELIEVE?

As with various other religious belief systems, Wicca has a system of beliefs that they follow and adhere to, and these include:

1. In terms of Theology: Wicca is basically a duotheistic religion and they believe in a God and Goddesses seen as opposite and polar divinities which are basically the embodiments of the life-force in nature.

2. In terms of the Afterlife: Generally, they do not believe in the Afterlife and they force emphasis on the current life. But, some Wicca practitioners do believe in reincarnation.

3. In terms of Magic: Magic to a Wiccan is basically a force of nature, and while many Wiccans does not know how witchcraft and spells work, they do believe it is nature working at its best.

4. In terms of Morality: They follow a strict code of "harm none", which basically states that Wicca does not allow the harming of any living thing.

5. In terms of the five elements: They believe in the four elements: Air, Water, Earth, and Fire, with a fifth element to balance and unite the four which is known as Aether or Spirit.

WICCA; THE PATH OF THE GODDESS

Wicca is an earth- and nature- honoring religion that celebrates the cycles of the year and the duality of divinity. It stresses living in harmony with all creatures and the earth. It honors a supreme power which is personified into male and female aspects as the Goddess and God. This is the Goddess and God that is contained in all nature and in ourselves.

Considered a mystery religion, Wicca is based on the pre-Christian spiritual traditions of England, Ireland, Scotland, and Wales. Its origins can be traced even further back to Paleolithic times when people worshiped a Hunter God and a Fertility Goddess. Still, it is considered a modern religion and not the Old Religion of those ancient times. Another way to put this is that Wicca is not THE religion but a religion sitting under the umbrella of Paganism much like Catholics or Methodists would reside under the umbrella of Christianity.

Wicca is practiced in a group (coven or grove) or solitary (by oneself). The goal of a Wiccan is to achieve balance and harmony within nature and oneself. This makes Wicca a highly individualistic religion. A large number of different sects within the Craft give the impression that no two groups practice the same way.

Thus, Wicca is a religion of clergy, not followers. Each person who seriously pursues the Craft, whether it be through study of a particular tradition, or through self-teaching and private learning, has the choice to become a priest or priestess of Wicca. Note that the word Wicca is an Anglo-Saxon word meaning "wise." Each Wiccan is striving to be wise within oneself and to have a direct connection with the divine power. Their personal faith is influenced by the religious experiences they have and often the experiences instill knowledge or religious truths in ways that are not fully understood by the individual.

Wiccas main tenant for ethical behavior relies on two basic premises. The Wiccan Rede or rule: "An it harm none, do as ye will ", or slightly updated: "If it harms none, do what you will." This means that as long as you don't do anything that will hurt anyone (including yourself) it is allowed. The other major premise is the Three-fold Law - whatever you send out into the universe, be it good or bad, you can expect to return to you threefold.

Wicca is compatible with the scientific method, and it is believed that all the Gods and forces are quite natural, not supernatural. Wicca encompasses a beautiful, satisfyingly natural way of life including the celebration of the solstices and equinoxes. These special times of year celestially signal the changes from one season of life to the next. It is about worshiping life and the love of nature and its power in all living things. Wicca believes divinity lives in everything natural thing and that karmic laws and reincarnation paths are present in the universe.

Wicca is an official, legal religion in the U.S., and a fast-growing one at that. Judges have ruled that witches must be allowed to lead prayers at local government meetings and that Wiccan convicts must be provided with requested "sacred objects" in order to perform spells and rituals within their cells.

So, Wicca is a religion which involves communion with the Earth, communion with a God/Goddess (or several of them if you're a polytheist), living in peace with yourself and others, and giving to those that gave to you. Witchcraft, by the way, is what Wiccans practice. Wicca is centered around the use of positive thought, positive action, and love of nature to create an atmosphere of positive energies which are then used for our own benefits.

Wicca teaches that there is certainly a higher power, namely the Goddess and God, often referred to solely as the Goddess, but that the Goddess is always attainable, for She is everywhere: in the tree, in the leaf, in the ant, within ourselves... To be a member of Wicca, one must seek rather than be sought after.

CHAPTER FOUR

GUIDANCE FOR WICCA BEGINNERS

Wicca beginners have a long, exciting and eventful journey ahead of them; a path brimming with greater wisdom and a new, more natural way of life. With so much ahead, it is no wonder that people can find themselves a little lost and overwhelmed. If you are lucky enough to live near a group or coven that you can join and be tutored by, then you will already be well on your way to a new lifestyle. However, for many Wicca beginners it is not as simple as that. Distance to loved ones and the influence of their own religious beliefs may prevent you from joining with others and openly declaring your new course.

Yet, you should never feel precluded from this wonderful religion, nor hindered in your ability to follow it. There is a wealth of information out there to learn from and nothing should hold you back from learning to honor nature and become at one with the world around you. However, seeing as this is what often confuses the Wicca beginner in the first place, here are some ideas and basic explanations to get you started and whet your appetite for more!

WHAT DOES WICCA REPRESENT?

This is a very personal thing and every Wiccan will give you a different account of why they believe and what it has brought into their lives. Every Wiccan will have a love of the earth and its universal elements. Water, air, fire, and earth will come to represent beauty, synergy, and power to every Wicca beginner. It is about recognizing, channeling, and connecting with the earth and its rich offerings - the gifts of Mother Nature. You will move and change along with the seasons and all of the associated festivals. Above all, Wicca is about peace and joy.

WHY IS IT A RELIGION?

While it is not a religion in the form that many people perceive a religion should take, Wicca is a religion due to its origins in Paganism. It takes on similar symbolism, belief systems, and of course Gods and Goddesses. It is not prescriptive like many religions are and Wicca will not tell you how to live your life, but it does help you to understand the world around you and make sense of the purpose of life.

WHAT IS THE DIFFERENCE BETWEEN WICCA AND WITCHCRAFT?

Occasionally, you will find different answers to this question, but as a Wicca beginner the details of this shouldn't concern you too much. To most, Wicca is the religious part of the lifestyle and those who practice it refer to themselves as Wicca or Wiccan rather than witches. They are more likely to be part of a coven or group and follow more rules. However, the name Wicca was introduced to distinguish it from the stigma associated with witchcraft and many aspects of the Wiccan and witchcraft life are very similar and the terms can be interchangeable.

THE WICCAN REDE

Wicca is a peaceful and gentle way of life that encourages respect. For this reason, selfish, manipulative, or sinister intentions are very much frowned upon. A small minority of Wicca beginners take an interest because they seek power over others, but will soon come across one of the very few rules, The Wiccan Rede - "An it harms none, do as ye will". This means you are largely free to practice as you please, however you must remember to embrace the earth's power for good over causing harm or hurt to others. This leads us to the Three-fold Law, which states that all that you do will come back to you 3 times as powerful. In other words, be careful what you wish for!

WILL I NEED TO WORSHIP ANY GODS OR GODDESSES?

No, but it is quite a significant part of the ideology and history. They also need to be understood as part of the worship of male and female. Many Wiccans will dedicate themselves to a single deity as they feel a strong affinity and can identify with particular characteristics. However, many of the Gods and Goddesses can be called upon to assist you in your work. As a Wicca beginner, it may be useful to try including as many deities as possible into your rituals to see if you feel a particular partiality to one or another.

WILL I HAVE TO PERFORM SPELLS?

No. Not all Wiccans believe in spell casting, so you should not feel pressure to do so. If you do find that you have an ability in this area, however, you will find plenty of information on spells for Wicca beginners on the journey to writing your own!

IS THERE SCRIPTURE FOR ME TO ABIDE BY?

The only book that Wiccans work from is a Book of Shadows and this is generally a very personal thing. A coven may have a joint one to work from, but very commonly you will have your own. It is a place for you to write your spells, keep notes, and make observations. Whether or not there has ever been a 'real' or ancient Book of Shadows, or a central text to work from, is a hotly debated topic; however, none has been proven to exist.

WICCA TRADITIONS

For some, Wicca is a solitary religion, something that we have taught ourselves through groups, books, or even the internet. Whether you grew up in a Wiccan family or were initiated the traditional way through a coven, it is important to understand all of the Wiccan traditions.

1. Gardenerian Wicca

Gerald Gardener's traditional way honors Cernunnos as the lord and Aradia as the lady. This path of Wicca is formal with skyclad worship and degrees of initiation with the covens having no more than thirteen members in each. The covens are led by a high priestess with a high priest. Gardenerians are not too impressed by self-initiation in other forms of Wicca because they believe that it takes a witch to make a witch.

2. Alexandrian Wicca

Founded in the 1960's by Alex and Maxine Saunders, Alexandrian Wicca is a formal, structured, neo-Gardenerian tradition. Both Gardenerian and Alexandrian Wicca are regarded as Classical Wicca.

3. British Traditional Wicca

This type of Wicca is similar to Gardenerian Wicca, also formal and structured, but mixes Celtic deities and spirituality as well.

4. Celtic Wicca

Celtic Wicca incorporates Celtic Gods and Goddesses with spirituality, green witchcraft, and fairy magic.

5. Dianic Wicca

This tradition is centered around the Goddess Diana that doesn't include gods. Dianic Wicca is often thought of as a feminist, even lesbian path, although there are male Dianic Witches. This path does not require initiations.

6. Faery Wicca

This Irish tradition is similar to Celtic Wicca focusing on green witchcraft and faery magic.

7. Teutonic Wicca

Teutonic Wicca incorporates deities, symbolism, and practices from the Nordic tradition, including Germanic and Norse cultures.

8. Family Traditions

Generations of witches having their secret practices and traditions.

9. Oxymorphic Groups

Satanic Wiccans and Christian Wiccans are not Wiccan, whether they mean well or not. It is a contradiction in terms!

Although some witches believe that each individual must have been taught the craft by a living relative before being considered as a hereditary witch, I believe that being a witch can be inherited from a grandparent who may or may not be living. The natural gift of witchcraft appears to skip a generation in many cases. There are countless reports of young witches receiving spirit messages from their ancestors, showing guidance on the witches' path, or discovering information that points to an ancestor being a witch.

10. Paganism

Paganism covers many faiths, one being Wicca. Wiccans respect others in their beliefs and value the freedom of worship for everyone. Wiccans are polytheists who incorporate various Gods and Goddesses into their rituals. Most witches believe in reincarnation, hence the representation of the seasons, birth, death, and rebirth.

Wiccans do not believe in hell or the devil. Wiccans choose to refrain from negativity by being positive. They hold an individual responsible for their own evil actions.

Many witches honor the Horned God, the Lord of Animals, and the Sylvan Lord of the Greenwood. He is otherwise known as Pan, Herne, or Cernunnos, a man with horns who is a great god of herds and fertility. Some witches believe in angels, some faeries, and some also believe in dragons. Each to their own.

SPELLS FOR BEGINNERS

Spells for beginners is a great way to get started on the path of Wicca and witchcraft. If you really want to be able to create powerful spells with little to no effort, you have to take the time to study, learn, and apply this information. The more in tune you get with the universe and the world around you, the more powerful your spells will become. A beginner casting a spell won't get the same results as someone who has been practicing for a decade. Here are some spells for beginners to start developing your natural power.

3 SPELLS FOR BEGINNERS:

1. To gain money

Get a cauldron. A large bowl will work fine, especially if you can find a metal bowl. A cauldron is used only for magical purposes because it is more powerful; however, it is not necessary. Fill the cauldron or bowl half full with water and position it outside where you intend to do the spell so that the light from the moon shines into the water. Sweep your hands above the water as if gathering the moons silver.

While doing this say:

"Lovely lady of the moon, bring me your wealth right soon.

Fill my hands with silver and gold.

All you give, my purse can hold."

2. To gain love

Start by getting some virgin olive oil and placing it in a dark, glass container. Fill it with rose petals and let it sit for at least seven days. Strain the oil from the petals and place back in the glass container. This can be used as an oil for any love magic you wish to do. You can also purchase a love oil at your local pagan shop. Get two red tapered candles and place them on a table side by side. Between the two candles, place an incense burner. Coat the candles in the love oil. When you are ready to begin, light the candles. Place a piece of charcoal in the incense burner and over it sprinkle dried rose petals. Recite the following incantation:

"Candle of power, candle of might,

Create my desires here on this night.

Bring me love, bring me a date,

Bring to me, my special mate.

Power, stream from this candle's fire.

Bring to me my heart's desire.

My words have strength, the victory's won.

So say I, this spell is done."

3. To lose weight

Get yourself a gold medallion and that has the likeness of a fish engraved upon it. You can find this at almost any good jewelry store. A small, plane medallion will do fine. If not, the power of the internet is brilliant.

Chant the following over the engraved medallion:

"Golden fish, I wear you,

In the belief that you will make me thin and beautiful.

Curb my eating, and let me eat fish and good food.

This will make me thin."

Now wear the medallion and go on a diet. The pounds will melt away with no struggle and sticking to your diet will be amazingly easy.

These are just a few spells for beginners that you can use right now. Remember though, to get the best results with spells, you must use them, you must learn, you must practice and grow. The wiser you are, the more powerful you are. The more powerful you are, the more powerful your spells become. A good teacher, program, or a truckload of books will help you learn and grow. Use these as a guide to develop your own unique spells.

CHAPTER FIVE

STEPS FOR BEGINNERS

To help you on your way to this exciting journey, here are 5 tips to getting started.

1. Many Wicca beginners cite spellcasting as one of their primary reasons for seeking out the faith. While there is no doubt that it is one of the most fun and life-affirming aspects of Wicca, it is not simple and you must realize that it's a skill as much as a way of channeling 'mystical powers'. You need to learn how to appreciate the powers that lie within you and what your personal style is. Set time aside for a simple, weekly spell session to monitor your progress and develop new ideas. Go for something simple like a spell for bringing positive energies into the next 7 days. See if you can tap into these feelings and draw the positivity of others towards you. This will give you a feel for energies, the spirits of the elements, the potential that lies within you, and last but not least, help you to see just how much fun performing magic can be!

2. The 5 universal elements are central to the faith and the Wicca beginner needs to start to introduce these elements into their life and spell work as soon as possible. These elements are the gifts of air, fire, water, earth, and the spirit (this represents you and your place on the earth). These elements have different powers and characteristics and you will need to start recognizing and respecting them. An important part of Wicca is the belief that expended energies will come back to you with three times the force, so it makes sense to ensure that the energy you send out there is always positive. Try to start making a habit out of giving something back to the universe when you can, from an act of kindness to dropping money in the charity box.

3. Seek out a quiet spot for performing your spell work or for your mediation and reflections. It is good to find somewhere where you feel both comfortable and safe. It will become part of the ritual itself, so be sure to choose wisely. As a Wicca beginner, you'll only need a few tools for a makeshift altar. A bowl for water, a candle, incense, and some salt will often suffice for a basic altar, but include something personal (a photo or favorite piece of jewelry, for example) until you start to feel truly at home.

4. Find local resources or groups (covens). You will be welcomed, initiated, and trained in the particular ways of the coven you have chosen. If you are lucky enough to have a variety of different traditions near to your home, then talk to them all to see if you are drawn to one more than the others. However, not everyone has such luxury. It is equally fine to consider yourself a solitary. For this, I recommend going online and joining groups and forums. You will find that people are happy to share their knowledge and experience.

5. Be realistic about what you expect to happen as a Wicca beginner. You will not be able to create miracles and you should not attempt to bend the free will of others. If you feel that these may be your reasons for wanting to embrace Wicca, you may need to reconsider. You will need to accept Wicca as a lifestyle practice and a faith, so be prepared to work at it. The rewards will come to you in time.

Just remember this, being a Wicca beginner is much like driving - everyone was a learner once! You may feel there's too much to take on at first, but take your time and enjoy as you start to reveal the possibilities of what is around you. You will soon start to adopt the Wiccan ways as a natural part of your life.

WICCA DAILY DEVOTIONS FOR BEGINNERS

When you follow a Magic path, your success in that path depends on your ability to focus charged energies and send them out into the universe to get whatever you desire. If you ignore your connection to Magic energy, it will weaken - as will your power. They are especially important for beginner Wiccans.

"Daily devotions" are things you do on a daily basis to strengthen your ability to control your inner Magic energy. A devotional routine helps to raise this energy daily, and can be performed at various times.

Think of daily devotionals as short rituals of energy. They strengthen your connection, and also bring positive energies into your life. Above all else, you want to pick a routine that is right for you and follow it every single day!

You can do all of your chosen devotionals at one time, or you can spread them throughout the day.

Find something that works within your schedule and follow it.

Your devotionals can be anything that brings positive emotion to your heart. It can be something as simple as making diary entries into your Book of Shadows every night before bed. In your Book of Shadows, keep track of where negative patterns are in your life and work to build on the positive ones in your mind as well as in the Book of Shadows.

Another devotional "mini" ritual you can follow is to spend at least a few minutes breathing, meditating, and visualizing positive things to create positive energy in your life.

Here is a list of some devotionals that you can do every day. There is not a need to do all of them, but pick ones that you feel most comfortable with:

Morning wake-up devotional

Connecting to the Lord and Lady

Connecting to the Divine, Infinite Energy

Greeting Devotionals to the Spirits or Elements around you

Connecting to Nature and the Earth Mother

Journaling

Food Blessing Devotional

Breathing

Meditation

Visualization Exercises

Playing with Energy

Remember, none of the devotionals you do should tire you out and you should never be in a situation where you dread doing them. You should look forward to them, so make sure you select ones that work best for you.

Most of the devotionals above are self-explanatory and you can create these devotionals any way that you wish. There are no "hard and fast rules" when doing your daily devotionals.

For now, I will walk you through the simple but powerful, "Playing with Energy" daily devotional.

Sit in a comfortable position. Take your hands, palms facing eachother, and briskly rub them together.

While you are doing this, start calling the energy from around you into your body. Hold your hands out in front of you, palms facing each other, about twelve to eighteen inches from your face. This works best for you to have a solid, dark background in the direction you are facing.

Focus first on your hands and sending the energy in your body out the palms. When you feel the flow is good and strong, shift your focus to just past your hands, at a point in the background beyond them. Can you see the ethereal, nebulous energy between the palms?

It may take some time for you to see it, but keep working at it, you will. Once you can see the energy there, concentrate on making it brighter and darker, increasing the flows and lessening the flows. Keep playing with the energy on a regular basis, until you get comfortable with how to manipulate it to do what you want it to do.

Once you have reached that point, start playing further with the energy. Form it into a ball, move your hands closer and further apart, seeing the ball change in size and intensity.

As you get the hang of each one (over days, not minutes!), try different shapes and sizes. Play with the energy and get comfortable with its existence. This is the same energy you use in order to cast magic. Seeing it in solid form, even if there is still an ethereal quality to it, helps to strengthen your belief and raise your levels of energy even higher.

CHAPTER SIX

WICCAN SYMBOLS

Wicca symbols have been with us for centuries, but are still as relevant to modern day Pagans and Wiccans as they ever were. Although there are some variations in the symbols from group to group, they are more often than not consistent in the conditions that they represent. This chapter discusses some of the most popular and potent symbols.

One of the most instantly recognizable of the Wiccan symbols is that of the pentacle - also known as the Witch's Foot. It is a 5 point star in a circle and each point represents (going clockwise and starting at the top):

1. The Spirit

2. Earth

3. Air

4. Fire

5. Water

The circle around them unifies and binds them all. This Wicca symbol is extremely important and powerful as it represents you and your place in the world with the elements - you are the spirit. Each has equal placing, and to take out one element would be to change the very nature of the union.

This is the symbol that Wiccans wear to identify themselves and other practitioners, making it the most identifiable mark of the Wiccan religion. It is worn with pride to mark the wearer's dedication to and respect for nature.

However, wearing this Wicca symbol is not without potential issues. There has long been a great misunderstanding that Wicca is somehow connected with dark forces, even Satanism. Fortunately, this could not be further from the truth. In fact, the wearer is stating that they are on a Magical path, but one which will take them away from evil, not towards it.

It signifies their desire to worship and honor nature in all its forms with respect for its great power. It is a personal pledge to give to nature and not to take from it unnecessarily.

Very similar to the pentacle is the Wicca symbol of the pentagram - the 5 pointed star of the pentacle, but which stands alone. This dynamic symbol represents the perfection found in nature and may be more familiar to you than you think - think of Leonardo Da Vinci's Vitruvian Man! Pythagoreans also viewed it as mathematical perfection. As misunderstood as the pentacle, it has also been viewed as having connectionns to dark forces, particularly when inverted.

There are signs that things are changing and Wicca is starting to shake off these old style views. In April of 2007, in America, it was ruled that the pentacle would be recognized and issued in military cemeteries and for tombstones, where previously this had been denied.

So, what do the individual Wicca symbols that make up the pentagram represent in themselves?

Earth is sometimes formed as a Wicca symbol by using the quartered circle, the perfect cross within the sphere, or alternatively as an inverted triangle with a horizontal line half way up. The symbol of the earth is a feminine energy - earth and Mother

Nature are often one and the same. It is the very foundation of our existence.

The Wicca symbol of air is almost the same as the triangle symbol for earth, but the triangle is upright. This element is all around us, essential for life itself, but also invisible making it an element that we can easily take for granted. This symbol urges us to honor and respect it. On Wiccan altars, incense is often used on the east to represent air.

Water and fire also use the triangle, but without the lines through them. Fire is upright and water is inverted.

The force and destructive power of fire cannot be mistaken. It is wondrous to behold when contained, but there is an ever-present sense that it could take control of your hands at any time. This Wicca symbol acts as both a reminder and a warning to take seriously the great force that nature can be.

Water is the deep and mysterious giver of life. Many people find that they have a great affinity with water and the sea, more so than the other elements as it seems to personify many human emotions and characteristics. It is hard not to stand and watch the ocean without feeling at one with it.

These core Wiccan symbols are only a few of the hundreds that you can study to further your understanding of both Wicca and the planet that we inhabit, instilling a respect that will make you feel more complete.

CAN ANYONE PRACTICE WICCA?

There is a misconception around who can practice Wicca and the concept is often confused with White Magic. As earlier clarified, Wicca is a way of thinking, a belief, a recognized religion, and like any other religion, anyone can practice Wicca. Wicca can be studied like any other religion, either in solitary or by joining a coven. A coven is quite literally a gathering of witches and much the same as popular culture has taught us, but without the green faces and warts.

In English Wicca culture, an initiation is required when joining a coven for the first time. When joining a Wiccan coven it is very important to remember that, as with the Christian churches, their ideas can be quite different from one coven to the next; it is also best to check that the coven is not a cleverly disguised cult that demands you give them everything, including the shirt from your back.

The best way to join is to research and talk to other people who are interested in Wicca, witchcraft, and all different types of Paganism. There is no better tool for this than the internet at the moment, particularly since it remains so very misunderstood. People are often surprised by the number of covens active in the world. Try looking for a local one! Alternatively, some people decide to practice Wicca in solitary and meet with other Wiccans or covens for rituals or festivities. The decision to go solitary or join a coven is a matter of personal choice.

Perhaps most importantly of all, when you approach a new philosophy, mode of worship, or any new group with different ideas, you must always maintain an open mind.

CHAPTER SEVEN

THE WICCAN CALENDAR

When practicing Wicca, it's important to know the Wicca calendar in order to practice the correct rituals during the correct time of the year. These Wicca holidays are normal pagan holidays in which rituals are done. This Wicca calendar explains what and when the different holidays are. Use this Wicca calendar in order to know when to worship and perform rituals. You may also wish to find specific rituals for specific holidays.

The great festivals or Sabbaths

1. Hallowe'en, also known as Samhain is usually observed on October 31st. The most accurate time to observe Samhain is the full moon before October 31st, however it is more convenient for people to observe on October 31st with the fast-paced world of today. Samhain is the time of the year that all of the souls and spirits in this world cross over to the other world and this is why we wear costumes today.

2. Lady Day or Candlemas is celebrated on February 2nd. This holiday is in celebration and hopes of the return of life. It is about celebrating the return of spring in the near future. The return of new life. This is a request for spring to come quickly so that plants and food can be planted and grown again. This is also a holiday for the maiden goddess to be welcomed back to the land, the homes, and the temples.

3. May Eve or Beltane is celebrated on May 1st. Beltane is observed to celebrate the return of the warmth and the sun. In ancient times, this was the time when herds were taken back to the mountains in order to graze on grasses. Bonfire was often seen across the landscape from one household and town to the next. Beltane marks the halfway mark of the suns journey between the spring equinox and the summer solstice. This used to be celebrated as the beginning of the new year.

4. August Eve or Lammas is celebrated on August 1st on the Wicca calendar. This holiday is observed and celebrates the first fruits of the harvest, and is the first holiday in the waning of the year. Lammas is a celebration of harvest, food, and abundant growth.

The lesser festivals or Sabbaths of the Wicca calendar:

The Rite for Spring is celebrated on the first day of spring. This holiday is exactly as its name implies on the Wicca calendar, the first day of spring. It is observed on the day of the spring equinox and is celebrated because it marks the first day that there are more hours of daylight than of darkness. It is the rite of birth and the beginning of the harvest year. It ends the long, cold winter and darkness.

Midsummer's Day is the first day of summer. This holiday is celebrated on the day of the summer equinox. It is the longest day of the year and marks the middle of the seasonal cycle. After this day, the days begin to get shorter and the nights get longer.

The Rite for Fall is the first day of fall and is celebrated on the day of the fall equinox. This represents the point at which the nights start to become longer than the days. This is the last day of the year that the daylight hours are longer than the nights. This also represents the beginning of the cold, dead season. Harvests are over and winter is on its way. This is time for reflection and contemplation of what is to come.

Yule is the first day of winter or the winter solstice. This is the holiday that the modern Christian Christmas replaced. Yule is the longest night of the year. It is a celebration of the beginning of the end of the cold season and the movement back toward light and warmth on the Wicca calendar.

This is a basic outline of the Wicca calendar. If you want to learn about rituals and rites done on these holidays or more about what each holiday represents, you will have to do more research. The scope of that topic is much more than can be covered here.

WICCA BASIC PRACTICES AND BELIEFS

Wicca mimics other world religions with its own rituals, seasonal "holidays", and belief system. The beliefs of the religion can vary by region, since there is no orthodox method of practice or central organization. There are, however, published teachings and works that most Wiccans adhere to.

The majority of Wiccans worship a God and Goddess who are considered to be equal, complimentary beings, and often are represented by the sun and moon. There is a trinity concept in this religion, with the Triple Goddess having aspects of the "Mother", "Crone", and "Maiden". Many members of Wicca concede that the Goddess had to predate her companion as she is the giver of life.

It is believed that both the God and Goddess are able to take form in the body of the Wiccan coven's Priests or Priestesses during the ritual. Though they believe in deities, the concept of an afterlife doesn't hold strong in the Wicca community. Reincarnation is a favored belief and traditional teaching.

Possibly the most adhered to text in Wicca is the Wiccan Rede, which states "and it harm none, do what ye will". This is interpreted as meaning that as long as a person's actions do no harm to anyone else, they can consider themselves free to pursue them. There is also the concept of the Law of Threes (also known as the Threefold–Law Return) that says whatever positive or negative actions a person puts out into the world, shall return to them threefold.

The magic rituals of Wicca are performed by a coven or group of practitioners. The rituals are usually begun by casting a circle and invoking the "guardians" of the elements and associated cardinal points: North (earth), West (water), South (fire), and East (air). The four elements are thought to represent every action and being on earth. The five points of the pentagram worn by those practicing Wicca stands for the elements and the presiding spirit.

After the circle is cast, prayers are made to the God and Goddess and spells may be cast. If it is at the time of a seasonal holiday, a special ritual may be performed. Tools a coven may have on hand for the ceremony include, a book of spells (Book of Shadows), an altar cloth, cauldron, chalice, wand, broom, candles, crystals, athame (ritual knife), and incense.

When the ceremony is finished, the God and Goddess are thanked for their participation and blessings, and the coven closes the circle.

The Book of Shadows mentioned above is a sort of personalized religious text for either a single practitioner or, more commonly, a coven. The contents are kept secret, but often contain such public domain works as the Wiccan Rede. What type of book is actually used varies among Wicca practitioners.

There are many "holidays" or seasonal observances in Wicca. Full moons (and sometimes new moons) bring about the ritual Esbat. There are also eight Sabbaths- four of which, the cross-quarter days, are larger than the others and relate back to ancient fire festivals. These are named Samhain, Beltane, Lammas, and Imbolc. The other, lesser celebrated festivals are the Summer and Winter solstices and Spring and Autumn Equinoxes.

DANGERS OF WICCA

Many beginners will be looking up the dangers of Wicca and I thought it would be a good idea to dispel some of the misunderstandings people have. Unfortunately, the people who think Wicca is dangerous in the first place aren't going to be convinced when someone tells them otherwise. So, the evangelicals can keep spreading their weird ideas, and people will still believe them.

Who knows, maybe someone will stumble upon this book and actually learn a little truth instead of ridiculous claims that other religious websites like to make.

So what are the dangers of Wicca? Well, none really. It's a religion much like any other, and that's about it. There is nothing particularly dangerous about it at all. There is no devil-worship nor any dealings with evil spirits. There is no devil at all, to be honest. Wiccans don't believe in such a being, so how can we get involved with that? That's a Christian concept, for the most part, that doesn't apply to Wicca.

Wiccans don't go around making blood sacrifices either. At least not usually. Curses and hexes may be part of someone's practice, but they are more often in the minority.

The main "danger" is that Wicca is dabbling in dangerous forces that are evil. The reality is that the energies of the Universe are neither dangerous nor evil, so that makes no sense at all. Are there dangerous spirits out there? I'm pretty sure there are, but getting involved with them is not part of the Wiccan tradition.

Now, if you are talking about teenagers dabbling around in some half-cocked version of Satanism, that is more movie-based than anything else, that's a whole other story. I'm not saying that's really dangerous either, just a different situation. Summoning a demon isn't going to work by reading some printout you found on a Wikipedia page. So, what's the harm?

Really, if you take a little time to find out what Wicca is about (worshipping a God and Goddess, honoring seasons, etc), you'll find very little to worry about. If you're worried simply because it's different, fear not. Many people feel this way about something new. Something new can be exciting which we tend to associate with danger. The reality is that Wicca is exciting, but also entirely peaceful. If someone you know is interested in Wicca, there is nothing to fear (except for the strange dabbling teenager types). True Wicca is not harmful, dangerous, or risky in any way.

CHAPTER EIGHT

MODERN WICCA

Many people argue that Wicca is a 20th-century neo-pagan faith or a new religion, while others say it has been around since the Ice Age and represents the old religion.

Wicca is both. Today's witches follow the traditions of old and are the shamans and healers of today. Witches practice sacred magic from the ancient art in today's world.

After Gerald Gardener's initiation by Dorothy Clutter buck aka Old Dorothy, into a traditional British coven in 1939, Gerald published books about the beliefs of British Wiccans. He wrote of their practices because he feared the religion was going to die out. Doing this broke the coven's seal of secrecy, but many people started converting to Wicca. This was the beginning of modern Wicca.

People still find it difficult to accept that witches are good and are still in fear of them. Witchcraft has adapted through time, but since the Burning Times,

Witches are now learning to live openly once more. There is no blood sacrifice or harm to any living animal anymore. Witches respect all living beings and honor them.

Every Wiccan is a witch, but every witch is not Wiccan. Wiccan witches serve the Goddess in any way they see fit using their abilities and personal circumstances. Wiccans do whatever they please and decide for themselves how they conduct themselves by obeying The Wiccan Rede.

Wicca is an Earth religion. Wiccans respect all people, are open minded to diversities, and consider everyone to be children of the same Mother, regardless of race, ethnic backgrounds, sexual orientation, gender, or status. These differences are not important to Wiccans.

There isn't a central organization or governing body, nor a supreme leader in Wicca. Wiccan temples are natural places of worship, be it a forest, beach, mountain, whatever, it really does not matter. What matters is that you share a strong connection with the place. Wicca is simply a collection of its witches with their beliefs and practices. Wiccans do not force anyone, man, woman, or child, to follow Wicca. They allow their children to decide for themselves if they choose to follow any religion.

Being a child of a Wiccan witch does not mean they are automatically Wiccan. They must choose to be. Many Wiccans wear a pentacle, mainly for protection. Wiccans choose their own lifestyle. Food is not restricted. Wiccans can eat meat or just be vegetarian. It is a free choice, just as all of a Wiccans life. Wicca is becoming a popular worldwide faith. Wiccans never try to convert anybody to their beliefs and never knock on doors or ask for money.

Believing in Wicca is a way of life, an organic religion, which celebrates Mother Nature. Wicca is a happy religion. It is also a personal and positive celebration of life. Anybody can choose to become a Wiccan. There are just two rules, abide by The Wiccan Rede, and more importantly, accept the Great Goddess into your life. Only then will you be ready to perform real magic.

CLOSING REMARKS

It can be hard in today's age and time to figure out what religion to believe in, let alone how to practice and study. In our western society, Christianity prevails, and that makes it hard to find good, quality information about other religions. Not to mention the fact that it is frowned upon to be a beginner Wicca practitioner. If you have decided to be a beginner Wicca practitioner, this information should help you to get started.

The beauty of Wicca is the freedom of will. The sole concept is that you may and can do as you wish, as long as it harms none. Now, this doesn't mean that you should do drugs, act irresponsibly, or do whatever you wish. At a deeper level, you need to develop the ability to see how everything affects everyone else. This, in the end, creates the need for you to develop an extremely deep sense of responsibility for your life, your actions, and how both affect everyone else. This is an absolutely necessary element to comprehend when you are a beginner Wicca practitioner.

The next step to think about when becoming a beginner Wicca practitioner is to sit and think about whether or not you really want to take the time and make the commitment to study and practice. I will be honest and upfront with you, Wicca takes a lot of time to research and learn. There are herbs, plants, energies, elements, symbols, tools for ritual, rocks, colors, spells, rituals themselves, holidays, covens, and a bunch of other information that you will have to take the time to learn about and understand.

There is no sugar coating it, becoming a beginner Wicca practitioner takes a lot of time and energy to gain a real understanding of witchcraft and all of the resources out there. Chances are that you will spend your entire life and only grasp a small fraction of it all. You must be willing to make the commitment if you really wish to become a successful Wicca practitioner. You can be one of those people who learn a thing or two and prance around pretending to be a Wiccan, but I have little respect for those types of people. Learn because you want to, not because you want to try and be cool or different in front other people.

Once you are ready to become a witch, Wiccan, pagan, or beginner Wicca practitioner, or whatever you wish to call it, you need to find someone who can teach you what you need to know about the knowledge and development process. Find teachers that can show you the ropes and take you step by step through the process of becoming a witch or beginner Wicca practitioner.

With all of the struggles that separate mankind in the world today, I maintain that religion should not be one of them. Instead, it should be a common ground that unites us all. Despite a cultures name for its God (or Goddesses) and the origins or mythic tales attached. I believe that God is most likely omni-lingual (fluent in all languages) and is present in all cultures.

I further suggest that any Almighty Being has better things to do than play monopoly among religious creeds. Education is the key to understanding, and there are many well-written, informative, and accurate books on Wicca available to assist you on your journey to enlightenment. Read. Learn. Practice. Grow. And above all else, believe in yourself.